Umräh Guidë B

Step-by-Step Umrah Guid

with

Important Rules for Female & Gu

Published By:
Islamic Book Store

e
y
oad

3876

Umrah Guide

is Ihram?

ans to declare something unlawful upon

ly referred to the clothing worn by a person
ah or Hajj.

in the context of Shari'ah refers to entering
hering to the prohibitions of even normally
with the intention of performing Hajj and/or
ing of the white clothing symbolises this state,
e is not entered into by wearing the sheets of

الإحْرَامُ عِنْدَ الحَنَفِيَّةِ هُوَ الدُّخُولُ في حُرُمَاتٍ مَخْصُوصَةٍ غَيْرَ أَنَّهُ لاَ يَتَحَقَّقُ شَرْعًا إلاَّ بِالنِّيَّةِ مَعَ الذِّكْرِ أَو الخُصُوصِيَّةِ .
وَالمُرَادُ بِالدُّخُولِ في حُرُمَاتٍ: الْتِزَامُ الحُرُمَاتِ، وَالمُرَادُ بِالذِّكْرِ التَّلْبِيَةُ وَنَحْوُهَا مِمَّا فِيهِ تَعْظِيمُ اللهِ تَعَالَى. (الموسوعة الفقهية الكويتية ج 2 ص 129 دارالس

Before Ihram

Before coming into the state of I

- It is Sunnah to take a bath.
- It is Mustahab :

> to trim one's mous
>
> remove hair from
>
> clip nails
>
> apply perfume

ي إلى مناسك ملا علي القاري ص 127 مؤسسة الريان)

يَّ صَلَّى اللهُ عَلَيْهِ وَسَلَّمَ تَجَرَّدَ لإِهْلالِهِ وَاغْتَسَلَ» وقال الترمذي «هَذَا حَدِيثٌ حَسَنٌ غَرِيبٌ»

يه وبقلم أظفاره ويحلق عانته كذا التوارث (المسالك في المناسك ج 1 ص 323 دار البشائر)

ـة البشرى)

هوَ الأَصَحُّ (حاشية ابن عابدين ج 2 ص 481 أبج أم سعيد)

اللهُ عَلَيْهِ وَسَلَّمَ، بِأَطْيَبِ مَاكُنْتُ أَجِدُ مِنَ الطِّيبِ حَتَّى أَرَى وَبِيصَ الطِّيبِ فِي رَأْسِهِ، وَلِحْيَتِهِ قَبْلَ أَنْ يُحْرِمَ» رواه النسائي

ble to wear two white new or washed
oth: an upper garment and a lower

ld wear slippers/sandals which expose
one/mid foot area where there is a
one.

---

1 مستحبات الإحْرام ...وليس إِزاراً ورداءً جديدين أيضين وَهُو أفضل أو غسلين (تحفة الملوك ج 1 ص 158 دار الكتب)

2(قَوْلُهُ فَيَقْطَعُهُما) أمّا لَو لَبِسَهُما قَبْل القَطع يَوما فَعليْهِ دَمٌ وَفِي أقَلَّ صَدَقَةٌ لُبَابٌ (قَوْلُهُ أسْفَلَ مِنَ الكَعْبَيْن) الّذي في الحَدِيث وَلْيَقْطَعْهُما حَتَّى يَكُونَا قَطعُهُمَا بَحيْثُ يَصيرُ الكَعْبَان أمّا لَو لَبِسَهُما مِنَ السَاق مَكْشُوفًا لا قَطع مَوْضِع الكَعْبَيْن فَقَطْ كَمَا لا يَخْفَى وَالنَّعْلُ هُوَ المِدَاس بِكَسْر المِيم وَهُوَ وَالمُرَاد قَطعُهُمَا بَحيْثُ يَصيرُ الكَعْبَان وَما فَوْقَهُما مِنَ السَاق مَكْشُوفًا لا قَطع مَوْضِع الكَعْبَيْن فَقَطْ كَمَا لا يَخْفَى وَالنَّعْلُ هُوَ المِدَاس بِكَسْر المِيم وَهُوَ وَهُوَ المَفصِل الّذي في وَسَط القَدَم كَذا رَوى هِشام عَن مُحَمَّد، بِخِلافِه في الوُضُوء فَإنَّه العَظْم النَّاتِئ أيْ المُرْتَفِع وَلَمْ يُعَيِّن في الحَدِيث أحَدَهُما لَـ احْتِياطًا لأنَّ الأَحْوَط فيما كانَ أكْثَر كَشْفًا بَحْر   (حاشية ابن عابدين ج 2 ص 490 السعيد)

قالَ: (وَلا يَلْبَسُ قَميصًا وَلا سَراوِيل وَلا عِمامَةً وَلا قَلَنسُوَةً وَلا قَبَاء وَلا خُفَّيْن) لأنَّه – عَلَيْهِ الصَّلاةُ وَالسَّلامُ – نَهَى أنْ يَلْبَسَ المُحرِم هذه الأَشْياء، فَإ رِداءَ شَقَّ قَميصَهُ فارْتَدى بِه، وَإنْ لَمْ يَجِدْ نَعْلَيْن يَقْطَعُ خُفَّيْن أسْفَلَ الكَعْبَيْن؛ لأنَّ هذه الأَشْياء تُخْرَجُ عَنْ لِبْس المَحيط وَهُوَ الّذي يَقدِرُ عَلَيْهِ وَالتَّكلِيفُ 144 دار الكتب العلمية

(قَوْلُهُ فَيَجُوزُ إلخ) تَفريعٌ عَلى ما فُهِمَ مِمَّا قَبْلَهُ وَهُوَ جَوازُ لُبْس ما لا يُغَطّي الكَعْب الّذي في وَسَط القَدَم وَالسُرْمُوزَة قِيلَ هُوَ المُسَمَّى بِالبَابُوج. وَذَكَر قُلْت: الأَظْهَر الأَوَّل لأَنَّ الصِّرْمَة المَعْروفَة الآن هي الّتي تُشَدُّ في الرِّجل مِنَ العَقِب وَتَسْتُرُهُ وَالظَّاهِر أنَّهُ لا يَجُوزُ سَتْرُهُ فَيَجِبُ إذا لَبِسَها أنْ لا يَشُدَّها مـ بَحيْثُ يَسْتُرُ الكَعْب الّذي في وَسَط القَدَم يَقْطَعُ الزَّائِدَ السَاتِرَ أو يَخْشُو في داخِلِه خِرقَةً بَحيْثُ تَمْنَع دُخُولَ القَدَم كُلِّها وَلا يَصِلُ وَجْهُهُ إلى الكَعْب وَقَدْ الْبَابُوج لِما فيهِ مِنَ الإِتْلاف (رد المختار ج 2 ص 490 السعيد)

Clothes of Ihram

Female Ihram:

- Women may wear an abaya, scarf, g
and shoes.

- The face must not have anything to
physically. However, a lady should
face with cap fitted with a veil hang
cap to prevent it touching the face.

«والقفازين»..(وتغطي رأسها) (إرشاد الشاري إلى مناسك ملا علي القاري ص 162 مؤسسة الريان)

الشيء متجاف جاز وفي النهاية إن سدل الشيء على وجهها واجب عليها ودلت المسألة على أن المرأة منهية عن إظهار وجهها للأجانب بلا ضرورة
ى وجهها شيئا وتجافيه (إرشاد الشاري إلى مناسك ملا علي القاري ص 162 مؤسسة الريان)

سُولُ اللهِ صَلَّى اللهُ عَلَيْهِ وَسَلَّمَ مُحْرِمَاتٌ، فَإِذَا حَاذَوْا بِنَا سَدَلَتْ إِحْدَانَا جِلْبَابَهَا مِنْ رَأْسِهَا عَلَى وَجْهِهَا فَإِذَا جَاوَزُونَا كَشَفْنَاهُ» (سنن أبي داود)

nah to perform 2 rak'at of Salah
e entering into the state of

rable to recite Surah Kafirun in
ak'at and Surah Ikhlas in the
k'at.

(وَيُصَلِّي) فِي مَوْضِعِ الْإِحْرَام (رَكْعَتَيْنِ) قَرَأَ فِيهِمَا مَا شَاءَ وَالْأَفْضَلُ أَنْ يَقْرَأَ بَعْدَ الْفَاتِحَةِ: قُلْ يَا أَيُّهَا الْكَافِرُونَ وَالْإِخْلَاصَ تَبَرُّكًا بِفِعْلِهِ – عَلَيْهِ الصَّلَاةُ وَالسَّ
شرح ملتقى الأبحر ج 2 ص 267 دار إحياء التراث

When should Ihram be worn?

- One must enter into the state of Ihram before passing boundary.
- Miqat is the outer boundary from where those wishing Umrah must enter into the state of Ihram.
- 5 Boundaries:
- 1) Dhul Hulaifah: north of Makkah
- 2) Al-Juhfah/Rabigh : north west of Makkah. (This is who come from the west)
- 3) Yalamlam- south east of Makkah.
- 4) Qarn al-Manazil: east of Makkah.
- 5) Dhat al-Iraq: North east of Makkah in the direction

وَأَمَّا مُحْرِمًا خَمْسَةٌ إِلَّا (ذُو الْحُلَيْفَةِ) بِضَمٍّ فَفَتْحٍ مَكَانٌ عَلَى سِتَّةِ أَمْيَالٍ مِنَ الْمَدِينَةِ وَعَشَرَ مَرَاحِلَ مِنْ مَكَّةَ تُسَمِّيهَا الْعَوَامُّ أَبْيَازَ عَلِيٍّ – رَضِيَ اللَّهُ عَنْهُ – ... عِرْقٍ) بِكَسْرٍ فَسُكُونٍ عَلَى مَرْحَلَتَيْنِ مِنْ مَكَّةَ (وَجُحْفَةُ) عَلَى ثَلَاثِ مَرَاحِلَ بِقُرْبِ رَابِغٍ (وَقَرْنٌ) عَلَى مَرْحَلَتَيْنِ فَتْحُ الرَّاءِ خَطَأٌ وَنِسْبَةُ أُوَيْسٍ إِلَيْهِ خَطَأٌ آخَرُ ... (وَالشَّامِيِّ) الْغَيْرِ الْمَارِّ بِالْمَدِينَةِ وَقَرِيبَةٌ مَا يَأْتِي (وَالنَّجْدِيُّ وَالْيَمَنِيُّ) لَفٌّ وَنَشْرٌ مُرَتَّبٌ (الدُّرِّ الْمُخْتَارِ مِنْ نُسْخَةِ حَاشِيَةِ ابْنِ عَابِدِينَ ج 2 ص 475 أيج أمم

أَبُو الزُّبَيْرِ، أَنَّهُ سَمِعَ جَابِرَ بْنَ عَبْدِ اللَّهِ رَضِيَ اللَّهُ عَنْهُمَا، يُسْأَلُ عَنِ الْمُهَلِّ فَقَالَ: سَمِعْتُ – أَحْسَبُهُ رَفَعَ إِلَى النَّبِيِّ صَلَّى اللَّهُ عَلَيْهِ وَسَلَّمَ – فَقَالَ: «مُهَلُّ أَهْلِ ... مُهَلُّ أَهْلِ الْعِرَاقِ مِنْ ذَاتِ عِرْقٍ، وَمُهَلُّ أَهْلِ نَجْدٍ مِنْ قَرْنٍ، وَمُهَلُّ أَهْلِ الْيَمَنِ مِنْ يَلَمْلَمَ» (رواه مسلم)

Boundaries

Mawaqeet

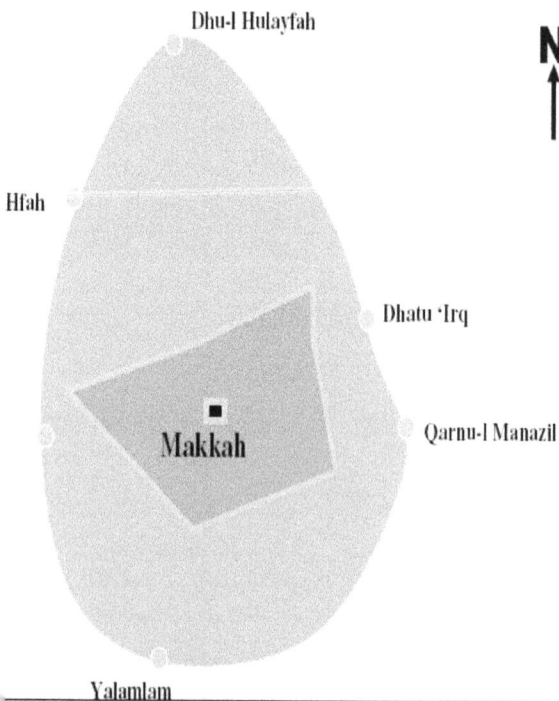

Dhu-l Hulayfah

N

Hfah

Dhatu 'Irq

Makkah

Qarnu-l Manazil

Yalamlam

Entering into Ihram

- Niyyah + Talbiyah = Ihram
- One may recite the following
  before reciting the Talbiyah:

إِنِّي أُرِيدُ الْعُمْرَةَ فَيَسِّرْهَا لِيْ وَتَقَبَّلْهَا مِنِّي

- One should then recite the T
  with the intention of coming
  Ihram.

(الهداية ج 2 ص 169 مكتبة البشرى)
الكتب

مَقَامَهَا مِنَ الذِّكْرِ أَو سَوْقِ الْهَدْيِ أَو تَقْلِيدِ الْبَدَنَةِ كَذَا فِي الْمُضْمَرَاتِ (الفتاوى الهندية ج 1 ص 222 الرشيدية)
إِنِّي أُرِيدُ الْحَجَّ وَالْعُمْرَةَ فيسرهما لي وتقبلهما مني (نخبة الفقهاء ج 1 ص 399 دار الكتب)

...he pilgrim's answer to Allah's call to Hajj.

لَبَّيْكَ اللَّهُمَّ لَبَّيْكَ، لَبَّيْكَ لَا شَرِيكَ لَكَ لَبَّيْكَ، إِنَّ الْحَمْدَ لَا شَرِيكَ لَكَ

...numa Labbayk. Labbayka La Shareeka Laka
...nnal Hamda Wan-Ni'mata laka wal mulk. La Shareeka Laka

...Your service, O Lord, here I am. Here I am, there is no
...here I am. Truly, all praise, favours and sovereignty are
Yours. There is no partner for You."

(، وَهِيَ لَبَّيْكَ اللَّهُمَّ لَبَّيْكَ لَبَّيْكَ لا شَرِيكَ لَكَ لَبَّيْكَ، إِنَّ الْحَمْدَ وَالنِّعْمَةَ لَكَ وَالْمُلْكَ لا شَرِيكَ لَكَ) أَيْ التَّلْبِيَةُ أَنْ يَقُولَ لَبَّيْكَ إِلَخْ كَذَا حَكَى ابْنُ عُمَ
(تبيين الحقائق ج 2 ص 10 إمدادية)
عَنْ عَبْدِ اللهِ بْنِ عُمَرَ رَضِيَ اللهُ عَنْهُمَا: " أَنَّ تَلْبِيَةَ رَسُولِ اللهِ صَلَّى اللهُ عَلَيْهِ وَسَلَّمَ: لَبَّيْكَ اللَّهُمَّ لَبَّيْكَ، لَبَّيْكَ لَا شَرِيكَ لَكَ لَبَّيْكَ، إِنَّ الْحَمْدَ وَالنِّعْمَةَ لَ

Rules regarding Talbiy:

Sahl ibn S'ad reports that the Prophet salallah
wasallam said,

*"When a Muslim recites Talbiyah, then verily every s
the ground around him recite the Talbiyah with hir
the Earth."* (Tirmidhi)

- The Talbiyah should be recited as much as
- Men should recite the Talbiyah audibly with
  others. Women should recite the Talbiyah
- The Talbiyah should be recited individually
  possible.

وَسَلَّم: «مَا مِنْ مُسْلِمٍ يُلَبِّي إِلَّا لَبَّى مَنْ عَنْ يَمِينِهِ، أَوْ عَنْ شِمَالِهِ مِنْ حَجَرٍ، أَوْ شَجَرٍ، أَوْ مَدَرٍ، حَتَّى تَنْقَطِعَ الْأَرْضُ مِنْ هَاهُنَا وَهَاهُنَا» (رواه الترمذي)
عد الْإِحْرَامِ وَكُلَّمَا عَلَا شَرَفًا أَوْ هَبَطَ وَادِيًا أَوْ لَقِيَ رَكْبًا وَكُلَّمَا اسْتَيْقَظَ مِنْ مَنَامِهِ وَفِي الْأَسْحَارِ هَكَذَا جَاءَتِ الْأَخْبَارُ عَنْ رَسُولِ اللهِ صلى الله عَلَيْهِ وَسلم

ص 204 دار الفرقان)
بل كل إنسان يلبي بنفسه)..(دون أن يمشي على صوت غيره (إرشاد الساري إلى مناسك ملا على القاري ص 146 مؤسسة الريان)

more emphatically forbidden.

, fighting, quarrelling are strictly forbidden.

intimacy with one's spouse.

o day clothes like Jubbah, shirt, trousers, t-

c. for men is prohibited.

e and fragrances is not allowed.

ody hair is prohibited; to comb, pluck, trim or

permitted.

ails is prohibited.

wear covering the shoe-lace area is prohibited.

فإذا لبيك ناويا فقد أحرمت فألق الرفث وهو الجماع وقيل ذكره بحضرة النساء والكلام الفاحش والفسوق والمعاصي والجدال مع الرفقاء والخدم وقتا والعمامة والخفين وتغطية الرأس والوجه ومس الطيب وحلق الرأس والشعر. (مراقي الفلاح ص 276 المكتبة العصرية)

(والجماع)..(ودواعيه كالقبلة واللمس) وفي معناهما النظر بشهوة (إرشاد الساري إلى مناسك ملا على القاري ص 165 مؤسسة الريان)

(قَوْلُهُ أَيْ الجِمَاعُ) هُوَ قَوْلُ الجُمْهُورِ شَرْحُ اللُّبَابِ – {أُحِلَّ لَكُمْ لَيْلَةَ الصِّيَامِ الرَّفَثُ إِلَى نِسَائِكُمْ} [البقرة: 187]– بَّرَ (قَوْلُهُ أَوْ ذِكْرُهُ بِحَضْرَةِ النِّسَاءِ قيل: وَهُوَ الأَصَحُّ شَرْحُ اللُّبَابِ، وَظَاهِرُ صَنِيعِ غَيْرِ وَاحِدٍ تَرْجِيحُ مَا عَنْ ابْنِ عَبَّاسٍ ثُمَّ. (رد المختار)

(وكل ما يواري الكعب الذي عند معقد شراك النعل) (إرشاد الساري إلى مناسك ملا على القاري ص 165 مؤسسة الريان)

Forbidden acts in Ihram

It is forbidden

- For a male to cover the head with someth[ing]
the head.
- For a male and female to cover the face i[f]
something is touching the face.
- To hunt or help in hunting.
- To kill lice.

Note: Any of these acts done will result in penalty

mistake or forgetfully.

أنّ السَّتْرَ يصيب رأسَه وَوَجْهَهُ كَرِهْتُ لَهُ ذلك لِتَغْطِيَةِ الرَّأسِ والوَجْهِ بِه، وإن كان لا يصيب رأسَه وَلا وَجْهَهُ فَلا بأسَ بِه ولا شَيْءَ عَلَيْه؛ لِأَنَّ التَّغْطِيَةَ شيئًا على رأسِه فإن كان شيئًا من جِنسِ ما لا يُغَطَّى بِه الرَّأسُ كالطَّسْتِ والإِجَانَة وَنَحْوِها فَلا شَيْءَ عَلَيْه، وإن كان من جِنْسِ ما يُغَطَّى بِه الرَّأسُ يكونُ هُوَ حامِلًا لا مُسْتَعْمَلًا، ألا تَرَى أنَّ الأمينَ لَوْ فَعَلَ ذلك لا يصيرُ ضامِنًا (المبسوط للسرخسي ج 4 ص 130 دار المعرفة) بِها على وَجْهٍ لا يصيب وَجْهَها، وقدْ بَيَّنَّا ذلك عَنْ عائشةَ – رضي اللهُ عنها –؛ لِأَنَّ تغطيةَ الوَجْهِ إنَّما يَحْصُلُ بِما يُمَاسُّ وَجْهَها دُونَ ما لا يُمَاسُّهُ لَيْسَ البُرْقُع؛ لِأَنَّ ذلك يُمَاسُّ وَجْهَها (المبسوط للسرخسي ج 2 ص 128 دار المعرفة)

r for purification or for coolness.

l soap. However, it is preferable not to remove dirt.

ses, glasses or a watch

py or diaper

to wrap yourself in a blanket. The whole body can be

he face and head.

, snakes, mosquitoes, wasps and flies.

قَوْلُهُ لا يَتَّقِي الِاسْتِحْمَامَ إلَخْ) شُرُوعٌ فِي مُبَاحَاتِ الْإِحْرَامِ وَفِي شَرْحِ اللُّبَابِ وَيُسْتَحَبُّ أَنْ لا يُزِيلَ الْوَسَخَ بِأَيِّ مَاءٍ كَانَ بَلْ يَقْصِدُ الطَّهَارَةَ أَوْ رَفْعَ الْغُبَارِ وَا،
وَغَسْلَ رَأْسِهِ وَلِحْيَتِهِ بِخَطْمِي) لِأَنَّهُ طِيبٌ أَوْ يَقْتُلُ الْهَوَامَّ، بِخِلَافِ صَابُونٍ وَدَلُوكٍ وَأَشْنَانٍ اتَّفَاقًا زَادَ فِي الْجَوْهَرَةِ وَسِدْرٍ وَهُوَ مُشْكِلٌ (الدر المختار ج 2 488
يَجُوزُ أَنْ يَرْتَدِي بِقَمِيصٍ وَجُبَّةٍ وَيَلْتَحِفَ بِهِ فِي نَوْمٍ أَوْ غَيْرِهِ اتِّفَاقًا (الدر المختار ج 2 ص 489 أيج أبج سعيد)
(وَشَدَّ هِمْيَانٍ) بِكَسْرِ الْهَاءِ (فِي وَسَطِهِ وَمِنْطَقَةٍ وَسَيْفٍ وَخَتْمٍ) زَيْلَعِيٌّ لِعَدَمِ التَّغْطِيَةِ وَاللُّبْسِ (الدر المختار ج 2 ص 490–491 أيج أبج سعيد)
(و) لا يَتَّقِي (خِتَانًا وَفَصْدًا وَحِجَامَةً وَقَلْعَ ضِرْسِهِ وَحَكَّ كَسِّرْ وَجَبْرَ كَسْرٍ وَحَكَّ رَأْسِهِ وَبَدَنِهِ) لَكِنْ بِرِفْقٍ إنْ خَافَ سُقُوطَ شَعْرِهِ أَوْ قَمْلِهِ فَإِنْ فِي الْوَاحِدَةِ يَتَصَدَّقُ بِشَيْءٍ
المختار ج 2 ص 491 أيج أم سعيد)
ولا شيء بقتل غراب واحد وعقرب وفأرة وحية وكلب عقور وفئل وبعوض وفئل وبرغوث وقرد وزلحفة وما ليس بصيد. (مراقي الفلاح ص 282 المكتبة العصر

Umrah

1. Ghusl for Ihram: — Sunna
2. 2 rak'ahs before Ihram — Sunna
3. **Ihram** with Intention and Talbiyah — **condit**
4. Tawaf — **requir**
5. 2 rak'ah after Tawaf — **neces**
6. Sa'y — **neces**
7. Halaq (shaving)/Qasar (trimming) — **neces**

ضان وهما النية والتلبية.وأما ركنها فالطواف.والإحرام شرط..(وواجباتما: السعي)..(والحلق أو التقصير) (إرشاد الساري إلى مناسك ملا على القاري ص

الساري إلى مناسك ملا على القاري ص 655 مؤسسة الريان)

akkah should be entered with humbleness with
conscious of the Grandeur of Almighty Allah.
t-seeing trip.

the city of Makkah, one will be taken to the
ggage in the hotel.

ly tired and it is not salah time, it is advisable to
forming Umrah. Umrah can take many hours in
the Hajj season and therefore requires plenty of

lling with the elderly and unwell, it may be a wise
n Umrah at night when the heat is less.

engaged in reciting the Talbiyah all the while.

(فيبدأ بالمسجد)..إلا أن يكون له عذر بأن يخشى على أهله وماله الفتنة والضياع..(بعد حط أثقاله) أي في موضع حصين ليكون قلبه فارغا (إرشاد السار
الريان)

قَوْلُهُ وَإِذَا دَخَلَ مَكَّةَ بَدَأَ بِالمَسْجِد) يَعْنِي بَعْدَمَا يَأْمَنُ عَلَى أَمْتِعَتِهِ بِوَضْعِهَا فِي حِرْزٍ (درر الحكام شرح غرر الأحكام ج 1 ص 222 مير محمد كتب)
ولا يؤخره) أي دخول المسجد والطواف (إلا لعذر) (إرشاد الساري إلى مناسك ملا على القاري ص 180 مؤسسة الريان)

Performing Umrah-Entering al-Masjid al-Haram

- Enter with the right foot reading the Du‘... salawaat upon the Prophet salallahu alaih...

- Proceed to the Ka'bah not as a tourist b... with utmost humbleness.

- Reach a place where the Ka'bah is clearl... which is not obstructing others.

- Stop and make du‘a. This is a very sacre... time for the acceptance of du‘a.

طا جلالة المكان مكبرا مهللا مصليا على النبي صلى الله عليه وسلم متلطفا بالمزاحم داعيا بما أحببت فإنه يستجاب عند رؤية البيت المكرم

ـة تلك البُقعة (وهَلِّل) تجديداً للتوحيد (ودَعَا) لأن الدعاء عند رؤيته مستجاب (فتح باب العناية)

The Ka'bah

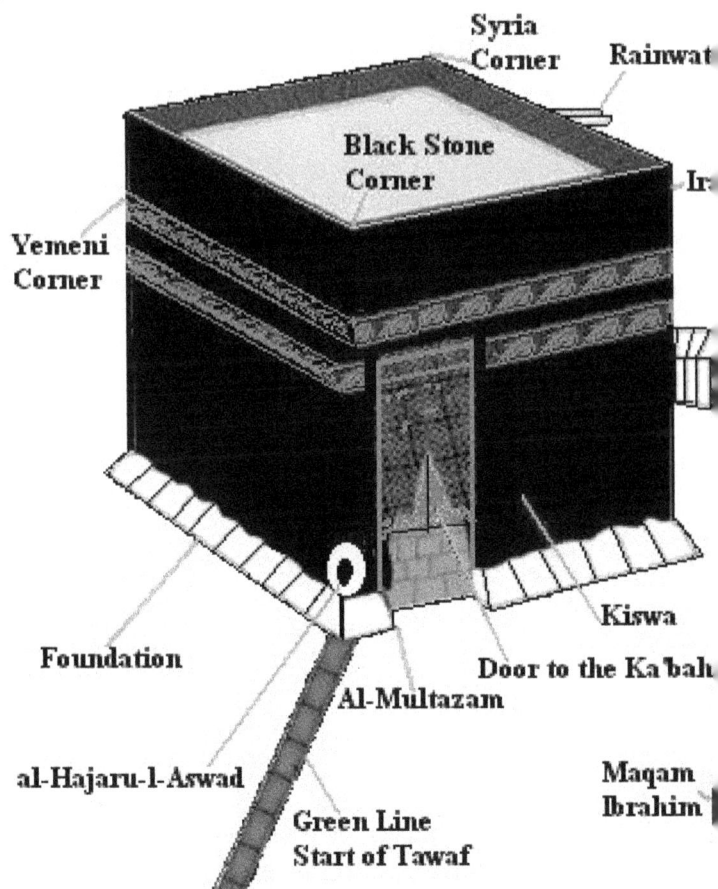

Syria Corner

Rainwat

Black Stone Corner

Ir

Yemeni Corner

Foundation

Kiswa

Door to the Ka'bah

Al-Multazam

al-Hajaru-l-Aswad

Green Line
Start of Tawaf

Maqam Ibrahim

compulsory part of Umrah and Hajj.

walk around the Ka'bah seven times.

(necessary) to have Wudhu when

Tawaf.

awaf, one should proceed to the corner

bah where the black stone is.

واجب للطواف بالكعبة. (نور الإيضاح ص 24 المكتبة العصرية)

(جاعلاً) قَبْلَ شُرُوعِهِ (رِدَاءَهُ تَحْتَ إِبْطِهِ الْيُمْنَى مُلْقِيًا طَرَفَهُ عَلَى كَتِفِهِ الْأَيْسَرِ) (رد المحتار ج 2 ص 495 أيج أبم سعيد)

قَالَ فِي الْفَتْحِ وَيَنْبَغِي أَنْ يَضْطَجِع قَبْلَ شُرُوعِهِ فِي الطَّوَافِ بِقَلِيلٍ اه فَلَوْ قَالَ الشَّارِحُ قُبَيْلَ شُرُوعِهِ لَكَانَ أَصْوَبَ فَافْهَمْ. (رد المحتار ج 2 ص 495 أيج وسنّته من حينِ الشروع في الطواف إلى فراغه، فإذا فرغَ من الطوافِ تركه، ولو صلّى ركعتي الطواف مضطجعاًكره ذلك. كذا في ((شرح لباب المناسك))

(ولا تضطجع) (إرشاد الساري إلى مناسك ملا على القاري ص 162مؤسسة الريان)

Preparation for Tawa[f]

- Men should uncover their right shoulder[s]
  Ihram sheet under their right arm. This
  Idhtiba'.

- Idhtiba' should be done shortly before t[he]
  Likewise, once the Tawaf is completed, [he]
  cover his shoulder again.

- Women must not uncover any part of th[eir]

- The recitation of Talbiyah ends with the [start]
  of Tawaf.

طَرَفَهُ عَلَى كَتِفِهِ الْأَيْسَرِ (رد المحتار ج 2 ص 495 أيج أبج أم سعيد)

الطَّوَافِ بِقَلِيلٍ اه فَلَوْ قَالَ الشَّارِحُ قُبَيْلَ شُرُوعِهِ لَكَانَ أَصْوَبَ فَافْهَمْ. (رد المحتار ج 2 ص 495 أيج أبج أم سعيد)

غ من الطواف تركه، ولو صلّى ركعتي الطواف مضطجعاً كره ذلك. كذا في ((شرح لباب المناسك)). (عمدة الرعاية ج 3 ص 353)

قاري ص 162 مؤسسة الريان)

th the black stone with the body facing it.   Now 2

o be done:

ise one hands like one does in salah whilst facing

e and say:

أَللهُ أَكبَر لَا إِلَه إِلَّا اللهُ

hands and saying the above, one will put the

to one's side.   This will always be done when one

Tawaf.

مُشِيرًا بِكَفَّيْهِ نَحْوَ الْكَعْبَةِ ثُمَّ يُقَبِّلُ كَفَّيْهِ، ذَكَرَهُ قَاضِي خَانُ (درر الحكام شرح غرر الأحكام ج 1 ص 222 مير محمد)

ن أمكنه الاستلام من غير إيذاء أحد، ولكن لم تمكنه التقبيل من غير ذلك لا يقبله، بل يسلمه، ويقبل يديه، (المحيط)

ذا أَتَى مَكَّةَ فَلَا بَأْسَ بِأَن يدخلها لَيْلًا أَو نَهَارًا وَيَأْتِي الْمَسْجِدَ الْحَرَامَ وَبِيدَأَ بِالْحَجَرِ الْأَسْوَد فَإِن اسقبله كبر وَرَفع يَدَيْهِ كَمَا يرفع في الصَّلاة ثُمَّ يرسلهما ثُمَّ يب

بر وَهَلل وَحمد الله وَصلى على النَّبِي صلى الله عَلَيْهِ وَسلم وَهُوَ رافع يَدَيْهِ مُسْتَقْبِلا بِوَجْهِه إِلَيْهِ (تحفة الفقهاء ج 1 ص 401 دار الكتب)

سْتَقْبِل (الْحَجَرَ مُكَبِّرًا مُهَلِّلًا رَافِعًا يَدَيْهِ) كَالصَّلَاةِ (الدر المختار من رد المحتار ج 2 ص 493 أيج أبم سعيد)

سْتَقْبِلُهُ وَيُكَبِّرَ رَافِعًا يَدَيْهِ كما يُكَبِّرُ لِلصَّلَاةِ ثُمَّ يُرْسِلُهُمَا كَذَا في فَتَاوَى قَاضِي خَانُ (الهندية ج 1 ص 225 الرشيدية)

Tawaf- Istilaam

- Istilam is to make some form of contact
  indirectly with the al-Hajr al-Aswad (bla
- If one can touch the black stone withou
  shoving or causing some difficulty, then
  place both hands on the stone and then
  in between. When kissing the stone, a nc
  be made.
- If one cannot kiss the stone, then merel
  stone and kissing one's hands will suffic
- Nowadays, due to the crowds, the above
  difficult.

فمه بين كفيه)..(ويقبله من غير صوت)..(إن تيسر)..(وإلا يمسحه)..(بالكف)..(ويقبله)..(وإن لم تيسر ذلك)..(أمس الحجر شيئا)..(وقيل ذلك

ديه مشيرا بمما إليه كأنه واضع يديه عليه)..(مبسملا مكبرا مهللا حامدا مصليا داعيا وقبل كفيه بعد الإشارة) (إرشاد الساري إلى مناسك ملا على

f- Istilaam

...it to be in line with the black stone facing

...tance, with the palms of both hands raised

...black stone, saying:

باسم الله الله أكبر

...to the black stone with one's palms, one

...is hands and put them down.

...e performed a total of 8 times: at the

... every round in Tawaf and after

...he 7th round.

ولأنَّ أشواطَ الطَّوافِ كَرَكَعاتِ الصَّلاةِ والاستِلامُ كالتَّكبيرِ فيُفتتحُ به كلُّ شوطٍ كما يُفتتحُ كلُّ رَكْعَةٍ بالتَّكبيرِ وَيُختَمُ الطَّوافَ بالاستِلامِ، (تبيين الحقائق ج ٢

Hajar al Aswad
(the Black Stone)

waf

...ing Istilam, one will begin Tawaf (circumambulation)

...lk briskly in the first three rounds. This is called

...sible to walk briskly due to the crowds, or due to one
... after family, one may walk normally.
...not do Raml. She will walk normally.
... be performed in the first three rounds. In the last
... male should walk normally.
...tba' will only take place in that Tawaf which has a

...af, one will not perform Raml or Idhtiba'.

يفتتح الطواف فيطوف حول الكعبة سبعة أشراط يرمل في الثلاثة الأول ويمشي على هيئته في الأربع البواقي من الحجر إلى الحجر ويستلم الحجر في كل شـ
ـم ذلك إذا وجد مسلكا (تحفة الفقهاء ج 1 ص 403 دار الكتب)
والأصل فيه أن الرمل سنة طواف عقيبه سعي، وكل طواف يكون بعده سعي يكون فيه رمل، وإلا فلا (بدائع الصنائع
لا ترمل) في الطواف (مجمع الأنهر ج 1 ص 285 دار إحياء التراث العربي)

Tawaf

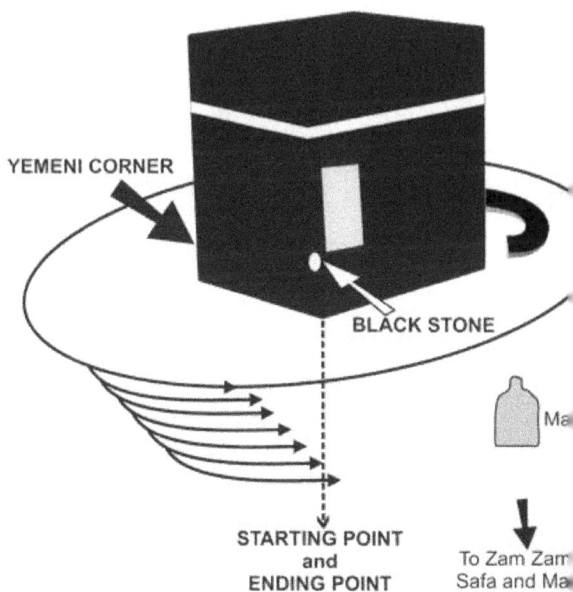

YEMENI CORNER

BLACK STONE

STARTING POINT
and
ENDING POINT

Ma...

To Zam Zam
Safa and Ma...

DIAGRAM ABOVE SHOWS SEQUENCE OF TAW...

alk around the Hatim and not cut through.

af recite Qur'an, Dhikr and make Du'a.

avoid talking whilst performing Tawaf.

not read loud in a manner which disturbs

to eat.

nk Zamzam in between if one feels thirsty.

(الطواف وراء الحطيم) (إرشاد الساري إلى مناسك ملا على القاري ص 217 مؤسسة الريان)

(وترك الكلام)..(وكل عمل بناي الخشوع) (إرشاد الساري إلى مناسك ملا على القاري ص 227مؤسسة الريان)

(ورفع الصوت ولو بالقرآن والذكر والدعاء) أي بحيث يشوش على الطائفين والمصلين (إرشاد الساري إلى مناسك ملا على القاري ص 234 مؤسسة ا

(والأكل).(وقيل الشرب) أي لا على ما كان طافة، ولا يَلزَمُهُ الاستقبال فَتح. قلْت: ظَاهِرُهُ أنَّهُ لَوْ اسْتَقْبَلَ لا شَيْءَ عَلَيْهِ فَلا يَلزَمُهُ اتمَام الأوَّل لأنَّ هذا الاستقبال للإكمَ

عَلَيْهِ حَيْثُ قال في فضل مُسْتَحَبّات الطَّواف: ومِنها استِئْناف الطَّواف لَو قَطَعَهُ أوْ فَعَلَهُ عَلَى وَجهِ مَكْروه قال شَارِحُهُ لَو قَطَعَهُ أيْ وَلَوْ بِعُذرٍ وَالظَّاهِرُ أنَّ

الجَنازَةُ أوْ المَكْتوبَةُ في أثنَاء الشَّوْط هَلْ يُتِمُهُ أوْ لا؟ لَمْ أرَ مَنْ صَرَّحَ بِهِ عِندَنا وَيَنْبَغِي عَدَمُ الاتمَام إذا خَاف فَوتَ الرَّكعَة مَع الإمَام وَإذا عَادَ للبِنَاء هَلْ يَبْ

والظَّاهِرُ الأوَّل قِياسًا عَلَى مَنْ سَبَقَهُ الحَدَثُ في الصَّلاةِ ثُمَّ رَأيتُ بَعضَهُم نَقَلَهُ عَن صَحِيح البُخَارِيّ عَن عَطاء بنِ أبي رَبَاح التَّابِعِيّ وَهُوَ ظَاهِرُ قَوْل الفَتْح

497 ايج ام سعد)

Miscellaneous rulings regarding Tawaf

- Whilst performing Tawaf, if one's Wudh Fardh Salah starts or one needs to take a is permissible to pause the Tawaf and th from the very place he stopped.

- One will not gesture to any other corner besides the corner with the black stone.

- It is mustahab to touch the al-Rukn al-Y corner) if it possible. If one cannot go the crowd, one should not gesture towa

- The al-Rukn al-Yamani should not be ki

بِالِاسْتِلَام هُنَا لَمْسُهُ بِكَفَّيْهِ أَوْ بِيَمِينِهِ دُونَ يَسَارِهِ بِدُونِ تَقْبِيلٍ وَسُجُودٍ عَلَيْهِ وَلَا نِيَابَةً عَنْهُ بِالإِشَارَةِ عِنْدَ الْعَجْزِ عَنْ لَمْسِهِ لِلزَّحْمَةِ شَرْحُ اللُّبَاب (رد

al-Yamani
(Yemeni Corner)

Completing Tawa[f]

- The Tawaf is completed upon making Istil[aam] Hajar al-Aswad (the black stone) at the end [of the ...] round. This will be the eighth Istilaam in t[...]
- It is Wajib to perform two rak'ats after Taw[af]
- The two rak'ats should not be performed i[n the ...] times for salah. These times are: After the [...] sunrise, at zenith, after the Asr prayer and [...]
- It is preferable to perform these two rak'at[s ...] Maqam al-Ibrahim. However, if there is n[o ...] space, one may perform these two rak'ats [...]

م عَلَيْهِ السَّلَام أو حَيْثُ تَيَسَّر عَلَيْهِ في الْمَسْجِد وَهِي عندنا وَاجِبَة (تحفة الفقهاء ج 1 ص 402 دار الكتب)

وَلا يُصَلِّيهِما إلَّا في وَقْتٍ مُباح (الجوهرة النيرة ج 1 ص 154 مير محمد)

الطُّلُوع والأستواء والغروب إلَّا عصر يَوْمه وَعَن التَّنَفُّل وركعتي الطَّواف بعد صَلاة الْفَجْر وَالْعصر (ملتقى الأبحر ج 1 ص 110 دار الكتب)

ajib element in Umrah. It is
l after the Tawaf. Sa'i is to walk
ne two hillocks Safa and Marwah.

ormed by walking between these two
ven times, starting at Safa and ending
.

where Sai is carried out is called

(وَالْعُمْرَةُ) في الْعُمُرِ (مَرَّةٌ سُنَّةٌ مُؤَكَّدَةٌ) عَلَى الْمَذْهَبِ وَصَحَّحَ في الْجَوْهَرَةِ وُجُوبَهَا. قُلْنَا الْمَأْمُورُ بِهِ في الْآيَةِ الْإِتْمَامُ وَذَلِكَ بَعْدَ الشُّرُوعِ وَبِهِ نَقُولُ (وَهِيَ إِحْرَامٌ
2 ص 472 أيج أم سعيد)

(ثُمَّ مَشَى نَحْوَ الْمَرْوَةِ سَاعِيًا بَيْنَ الْمِيلَيْنِ الْأَخْضَرَيْنِ) الْمُتَّخَذَيْنِ في جِدَارِ الْمَسْجِدِ (وَصَعِدَ عَلَيْهَا وَفَعَلَ مَا فَعَلَهُ عَلَى الصَّفَا يَفْعَلُ هَكَذَا سَبْعًا يَبْدَأُ بِالصَّفَا
501 أيج أم سعيد)

Preparing for Sa'

- After performing the two rak'at
  Tawaf, one should go in line wi
  Hajar al-Aswad again and do Is
  the commencing of Sa'i.

- He will then exit the Masjid and
  towards the Safa hillock which i
  the mas'aa (place where Sa'i is o

يستلمه إن أمكنه أو يستقبله بِوَجْهِه وَيكبر ويهلل ويحمد الله تَعَالَى على مَا ذكرنَا حَتَّى يكون افْتِتَاح السَّعْي باستلام الْحجر كَمَا يكون افْتِتَاح الطّواف

f the mas'aa (where

rformed)

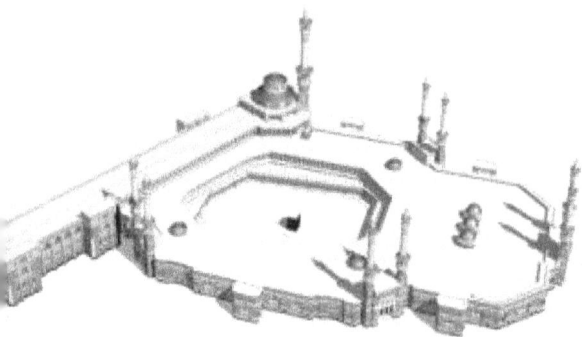

Aerial view of Mas'a

to the Safa hillock ensuring one is standing on
Safa.

h and one will say

الله أكبر لا إله إلا الله

"Allahu Akbar la ilaha illah"

n make Du'a to Allah.

ards Marwah.

n light approaches, a male should run until the
t.

يخرج من باب الصفاء أو من أي باب تيسَّر لَهُ فَيَبْدَأ بالصفا فيصعد عَلَيْهَا ويقف من حَيْثُ يرى الْبَيْت ويحول وَجهه إِلَى الكعبة ويكبر ويهلل ويحمد وسلم ويسأل الله تَعَالَى خَوَائِجه

ويرفع يَدَيْهِ وَيجْعَل بطُون كفيه نَحْو السَّمَاء

ثُمَّ يهْبط مِنْهَا نَحْو الْمَرْوَة مَاشِيا على هيئته حَتَّى يَنْتَهِي إِلَى بطن الْوَادي فَإِذا كَانَ عِنْد الْميل الْأَخْضَر سعى فِي بطن الْوَادي سعيا حَتَّى يُجَاوز الْميل الْأَ صعد مِنْهَا يقف وَيَسْتَقْبِل بِوَجْهِهِ الْكَعْبَة وَيفْعل مِثْلَمَا فعل على الصَّفَا وَيطوف بَينهمَا سَبْعَة أَشْوَاط يَبْدَأ بالصفا وَيخْتم بالمروة يعد الْبَدَاءَة شوطا وَالْعود شو
الفقهاء ج 1 ص 402–403 دار الكتب)

Performing Sa'i

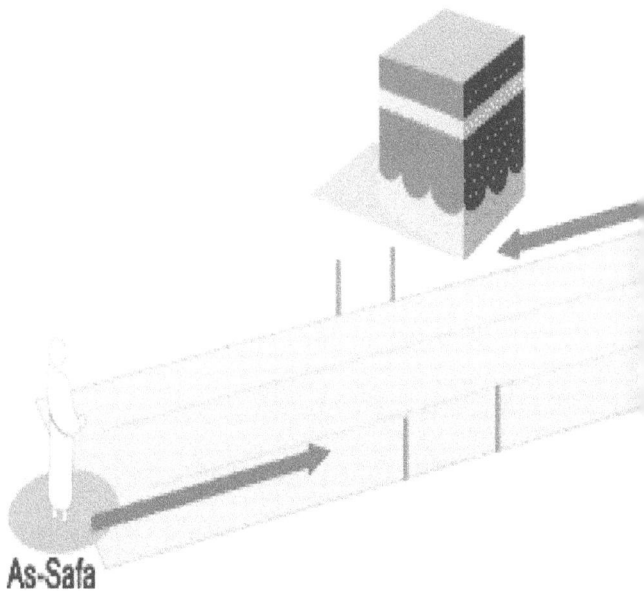

As-Safa

not run between the two green lights at the

on reaches Marwah, he has completed one lap.

one will again face towards the Qiblah and say

ألله أكبر لا إله إلا الله

"Allahu Akbar la ilaha illah"

then make Du'a to Allah.

Du'a, one will head again towards Safa.

eatedly do this until he finishes the seventh lap

Marwah.

(قَوْلُهُ: وَلا تَسْعَى بَيْنَ الْمِيلَيْنِ) أَيْ فَتَمْشِي بَيْنَهُمَا عَلَى هِيئَتِهَا كَبَاقِي السَّعْيِ بَيْنَ الصَّفَا وَالْمَرْوَةِ؛ لِأَنَّ سَعْيَهَا بَيْنَ الْمِيلَيْنِ مُحَلٌّ بِالسَّتْرِ أَوْ؛ لِأَنَّ أَصْلَ الْمَشْرُ

شرح غرر الحكام ج 1 ص 324 مير محمد)

Safa Mountain

بداية الصفا
SAFA START
شروع اسفا

Completing Sa'

- After standing on Marwah the seve
  making Du'a, it is Mustahab to per
  rak'ats in the Masjid.

سَبْعًا يَبْدَأُ بِالصَّفَا وَيَخْتِمُ) الشَّوْطَ السَّابِعَ (بِالْمَرْوَةِ) فَلَوْ بَدَأَ بِالْمَرْوَةِ لَمْ يَعْتَدَّ بِالْأَوَّلِ هُوَ الْأَصَحُّ وَنُدِبَ خَتْمُهُ بِرَكْعَتَيْنِ فِي الْمَسْجِدِكَخَتْمِ الطَّوَافِ (الدر

(سعيد)

ecessary to have Wudhu when

ng Sa'i.

ld engage in Dhikr and Du'a.

arts or one needs to take a break,

issible to continue from where

d.

(وأما الطهارة عن الحدث الأصغر في الطواف) وكذا طهارة البدن والثوب والمكان (فليست بشرط لصحة السعي) (إرشاد الساري إلى مناسك ملا ع

لو أقيمت الصلاة المكتوبة أو الجنازة وهو يسعى ينبغي أن يصلي ويبني وكذا لو عرض له مانع أو باعث (إرشاد الساري إلى مناسك ملا على القاري

Al-Tahleeq (Shaving) and al-Taqseer (Trimming)

- Shaving or trimming the hair is Wajib for men t[...]
  Ihram.
- Shaving the head is better than trimming the ha[...]
- All the hair on the head should be shaved or tri[...]
- It is permissible to cut one's own hair or go to t[...]
- A woman must only cut an inch of her hair and [...]
  can cut it herself.
- Once a person cuts his/her hair, they are free fr[...]
  Ihram and the Umrah is complete.

ا، وَذَلِكَ أَقَلُّ أَشْوَاطِ الطَّوَافِ وَالسَّعْيِ وَالحَلْقِ أَوِ التَّقْصِيرِ (رد المحتار ج 2 ص 473 أيج أبم سعيد)
خُرُجُ مِنْهَا (رد المحتار ج 2 ص 472–473 أبج أبم سعيد)
رَسُولُ اللهِ – صَلَّى اللهُ عَلَيْهِ وَسَلَّمَ – أَنَّهُ نَهَى النِّسَاءَ عَنِ الحَلْقِ وَأَمَرَهُنَّ بِالتَّقْصِيرِ عِنْدَ الخُرُوجِ مِنَ الإِحْرَامِ، وَلِأَنَّ الحَلْقَ فِي حَقِّهَا مُثْلَةٌ، وَالمُثْلَةُ حَرَامٌ،
لِلرَّجُلِ لِحْيَتَهُ عِنْدَ الخُرُوجِ مِنَ الإِحْرَامِ لا تَحْلِقُ هِيَ رَأْسَهَا (المبسوط ج 4 ص 33 دار المعرفة)
حِقُهَا فَلا تُؤمَرُ بِهِ وَإِنَّمَا عَلَيْهِنَّ القَصِيرُ..وَيَكْفِيهَا قَدْرُ أَنْمُلَةٍ تَأخُذُ مِن رَأْسِهَا (المسالك في المناسك ج 1 ص 582 دار البشائر)

tant rulings for

es

The prohibited actions during menstruation

- 8 acts are not permissible whilst experien[cing] menses:

1) Performing Salah
2) Fasting
3) Reciting the Qur'an
4) Touching the Qur'an
5) Entering a masjid
6) Performing Tawaf
7) Intimate relations
8) Fulfilling one's passions by using the ar[ea between the] navel and knees without a barrier in be[tween]

الطواف.

الركبة. (نور الإيضاح ص 38 مكتبة العصرية)

will not perform the two rak'ats
fore Ihram if she is in her menses.

will merely recite the Talbiyah and
ah to come into the state of Ihram.

can recite the Talbiyah and any Du'a
ses.

cannot recite the Qur'an, perform
the masjid or perform Tawaf in her

Umrah

- If a woman is experiencing [
  menses, she will not perform
  Salah or Tawaf.
- A woman will not enter al-M
  Haram until after her mense
  complete and she has taken

an entered into Ihram and she
iencing her menses, then she will
rm the Umrah until after she
free of her menses.

ave to remain in the state of
il she performs Umrah.

مسائل رفعت قاسمي ج 5 ص 109 (حامد کتب)

- If she could not perform Umrah du
  Hajj days starting, and she is still in
  then she should release herself from
  of Umrah and now enter into the s
  Ihram for Hajj.

- A woman will have to perform Qad
  Umrah and give a dam penalty in th

- Umrah should not be performed be
  9th-13th Dhul Hijjah by men and wo

10 (حامد کتب)

h Completed

rah is now complete!

ow free from all the prohibitions

Allah in the most sacred place
to Him with your heart.

.com/pod-product-compliance
up UK Ltd.
nes, MK11 3LW, UK
25
B/421

APOLOGETICS

APOLOGETICS

The Truth, The Whole Truth, And Nothing But The Truth

Greg L. Bahnsen

First published online in audio format by the Bahnsen Institute in 2023. Transcribed and republished with permission.

The transcript was lightly edited for ease of reading by the vice-chairman of the Bahnsen Institute, Rev. Christian McShaffrey, M.Div.

Cover Photo: Daniel Tadevosyan

First Printing, 2024

The following primer on presuppositional apologetics in the tradition of Cornelius Van Til was adapted from an oral presentation offered by Dr. Greg Bahnsen during an informal debate with Dr. R.C. Sproul in 1977 at the Reformed Theological Seminary in Jackson, Mississippi. See the appendix for more information about the author and the exchange.

A digitally remastered recording of the debate is available as a free download from the Bahnsen Institute. Visit *bahnseninstitute.com* or use the QR code to proceed directly to the relevant page.

Apologetics: Considered Negatively

As we think about the task of Christian apologetics (and the presuppositional method in particular), it might be helpful first to clear the way a bit by explaining what apologetics *is not*.

First, *apologetics is not mere persuasion*. Much of the popular literature in the area of theistic and anti-theistic apologetics consists of highly polemical and emotional efforts at converting others.

To be sure, it is often our duty to seek to convert an opponent to our position. These efforts, however, too frequently substitute mere attempts at psychological persuasion for careful and fair argumentation. Both believers and unbelievers stand guilty in this regard.

Unfortunately, arguments based on poor logic can often prove psychologically effective in convincing people of the truth of a particular position. Conversely, sound arguments can sometimes prove ineffective. Consequently, we may find ourselves confronted by a moral dilemma when we discover that certain bad arguments and glib slogans will be found more convincing by a larger audience than what, in fact, really are *good* arguments.

When, on top of this, we judge the issue that is being disputed to be one of high importance in our lives — such as is the case with apologetics — we are especially tempted to put forth these bad arguments in the service of the truth.

The Christian apologist ought to be the one person on earth who will resist this temptation. We only dishonor the truth — and ultimately dishonor the Lord of truth — when we use fraudulent and specious forms of argument in promoting the truth.

We may persuade a lot of people to become Christians on the basis of very bad arguments, when in reality our task as apologists is to find good arguments that will not be exposed later as fraudulent when someone with greater intellectual talent comes along and exposes our fallacies.

Secondly, *apologetics does not deal in mere probabilities*. We have been called to give a reasoned defense of the *conviction*, or the hope that is in us according to 1 Peter 3:15. When we base our thinking on the apostolic word, we can know assuredly (*asphalōs*, Acts 2:36), and without any doubt whatsoever, that God has made Jesus both Lord and Christ.

This is because the gospel comes to us that we "may have certainty concerning the things [we] have been taught" (Luke 1:4). "Our gospel came to you not only in word, but also in power and in the Holy Spirit and with full conviction" (1 Thessalonians 1:5). The Greek word there (*plērophoria*) means full conviction, assurance, certainty (i.e., perfect faith, not marred by any doubts whatsoever).

The Bible also speaks of our "full assurance of understanding" (Colossians 2:2) and our "full assurance of hope" (Hebrews 6:11). Abraham is called the father of the faithful and, with respect to his faith, Paul says that he "did not weaken in faith," but was "fully convinced" with respect to God's word of promise (Romans 4:19, 21) and thus, the epistle to the Hebrews invites us to draw near unto God "with a true heart in full assurance of faith" and also urges us to "hold fast the confession of our hope without wavering" (10:22–23).

In Christ, we surpass all human probabilities and have bold access to God through confident faith (cf. Paul's prayer in Ephesians 3:14–19). So while the confidence of the godless is as flimsy as a spider's web (Job 8:14), there is, in the fear of the Lord, strong confidence (Proverbs 14:26).

The reason the Proverbs can assert this is because the fear of the Lord is the beginning of all knowledge (1:7). We who put our confidence in Jehovah may "know the certainty of the words of truth" (cf. 22:21, ASV) and thus, I maintain that it is wrong to think that certainty in epistemological matters is limited to formal logic and mathematics.

Certainty (i.e., full certainty, full confidence, without doubt, without yielding, without qualification) pertains to the matters of the Christian faith.

John's emphatic purpose in writing his first

epistle was that his readers might have confident knowledge of their salvation. Therefore, the *Westminster Confession of Faith* teaches us that believers "may, in this life, be certainly assured that they are in the state of grace" (18.1) and continues to make very clear its meaning when it says, "This certainty is not a bare conjectural and probable persuasion grounded upon a fallible hope; but an infallible assurance of faith founded upon the divine truth" (18.2).

Apologetics, then, is a discipline that deals with the hope that is in us (i.e., with demonstrations that yield full conviction). Apologetics does not deal in mere probabilities, but in "the full assurance of faith" (Hebrews 10:22).

As a brief aside, talk of "moral persuasion" or "moral certainty" at this point is simply a cop-out. For whatever that strange state of mind is supposed to be, it is not compatible with mere rational probability. Moral assurance is to be based on the apprehended strength of the evidence and, as all philosophers who have spoken of this suspicious state of mind have said, it is to be proportioned to the certainty of the evidence itself.

Apologetics is not mere persuasion, and it also does not deal in mere probabilities. It is important to underscore this point. We are not simply trying to persuade people. We are interested in the true grounds for our Christian faith. We are not talking about what is *probably* true, but rather what is fully and unyieldingly true.

Apologetics: Considered Positively

The Apostle Paul asks in 1 Corinthians 1:20, "Where is the one who is wise? Where is the scribe? Where is the debater of this age? Has not God made foolish the wisdom of the world?" In that one phrase, we find the battle cry of presuppositional apologetics: "Has not God made foolish the wisdom of the world (age)?"

Our apologetical procedure is twofold according to Proverbs 26:4–5. It is how we show the foolishness of the wisdom of this age:

> **Answer not a fool according to his folly,**
> **lest you be like him yourself.**
> **Answer a fool according to his folly,**
> **lest he be wise in his own eyes.**

The Proverb first says, "Answer not a fool according to his folly, lest you be like him yourself." That is, do not answer a fool according to *his* approach to things, or according to his folly, or according to his assumptions or presuppositions (if I can import that term). You are not to answer it that way, because then you are going to be like him. You will be like an enemy behind the lines.

Yet the Proverb continues, "Answer a fool according to his folly." This, by the way, is not a violation of the law of contradiction. Instead, it is simply setting forth a twofold procedure for defending the faith.

First, *don't* answer an opponent according to his folly, lest you fall into the same pit with him. Then, *do* answer him according to his folly. Why? "Lest he be wise in his own conceits."

You must show the unbeliever that he has no ground for his conceited knowledge. You must show him that God has made foolish the wisdom of this age.

Paul says in Colossians 2:3 that "in Christ are hidden all the treasures of wisdom and knowledge."

Yes, all the treasures of wisdom and knowledge (be they pertaining to logic, or to causality, or to natural science, or morality, or whatsoever)!

All knowledge is deposited in Christ and thus Paul is able to say that since all the treasures of wisdom and knowledge are in Christ, you should see to it that no one "robs you" through what he calls "vain philosophy and empty deception" (paraphrasing vs. 8). Paul describes "vain" philosophy in terms of thinking that is "according to the traditions of men" (i.e., according to the elementary principles of worldly learning, *rather than* according to Christ).

The presuppositional model of apologetics instructs us not to answer a fool according to his elementary principles of learning, because we will become like him. Instead, we are called to answer according to *our own* presuppositions — those that are according to Christ — for then we will be able to conclude with Paul that "God made foolish the wisdom of this world."

The nature of the apologetical situation can be stated briefly in this way: First, the controversy between the believer and the unbeliever is *in principle* an antithesis between two complete systems of thought, involving ultimate commitments and ultimate assumptions.

Second, even the laws of thought and the laws of methodology, along with one's factual evidence, will be accepted and evaluated in light of those governing presuppositions.

Third, all chains of argumentation (especially over matters of ultimate personal importance) will trace back to, and will depend on, starting points which are taken as self-evident. Thus, *circularity* in debate will be *unavoidable*. That is not, however, to say that all circles are intelligible or valid.

Fourth, and because this is the case, appeals to logic, appeals to fact, and appeals to personality may be necessary in apologetics, but they are never apologetically adequate. What is needed are not piecemeal replies, probabilities, or isolated evidences, but rather an attack upon the underlying presuppositions of the unbeliever's entire system of thought.

Finally, and according to Scripture, the unbeliever's system of thought can be characterized as follows:

By nature, every unbeliever bears the image of God (cf. Genesis 1:26–27), and is therefore *inescapably religious*. His heart testifies continually to him, as does also the clear revelation of God around him, that God exists, and that he has a certain character.

Further, the unbeliever exchanges the truth of God for a lie (cf. Romans. 1:18–25). He is therefore a fool who refuses to begin his thinking with reverence for the Lord. He will not build on Christ's self-evidencing words. He will instead suppress the unavoidable revelation of God in nature.

Because the unbeliever delights not in understanding but chooses to serve the creature rather than the Creator, he is self-confidently committed to his own ways of thought; being convinced that it is not possible that he might be fundamentally wrong. The unbeliever flaunts perverse thinking and challenges the self-attesting Word of God.

Consequently, the unbeliever's thinking results in ignorance. In his darkened, futile mind, he actually hates knowledge and can gain only a "knowledge falsely so-called," as Paul says in 1 Timothy 6:20 (ASV).

To the extent that he actually knows anything, it is due to his unacknowledged dependence upon suppressed truth — the suppressed truth of God within him. This renders the unbeliever *intellectually schizophrenic*. Because of his espoused way of thinking, he is actually opposing himself, and showing the need for a radical change of mind so that he might gain a genuine knowledge of the truth.

Nonetheless, the unbeliever's ignorance is still a *culpable* ignorance, He is "without excuse" for his rebellion against God's self-revelation (Romans 1:20) and he is (literally) "without an apologetic" (i.e., without a defense for his thoughts).

The unbelief of the non-Christian does not stem from a lack of actual evidence, but from his refusal to submit to the authoritative Word of God from the very beginning of his thinking.

Apologetics: God's Requirement

Having considered the intellectual situation into which we are thrust as "defenders" of the faith, it is necessary that we now consider the question, "What are the requirements of us as apologists?"

First of all, I would say that the apologist must have a proper *attitude*. He cannot be arrogant or quarrelsome. He must, with humility and respect ("meekness and fear" per 1 Peter 3:15), set forth his arguments in a gentle and peaceable fashion.

Second, the apologist must have the proper *starting point*. He must take God's Word as his self-evidencing presupposition. He must think God's thoughts after him, rather than attempting to be neutral in his debate. He must view God's Word as more sure than even his personal experience of the facts.

Third, the apologist must adopt a proper *method*. Working on the unbeliever's unacknowledged presuppositions, and being firmly grounded in his own presuppositions, the apologists must aim to cast down every high imagination that is exalted against the knowledge of God by aiming to bring every thought — his own as well as his opponent's — captive to the obedience of Christ (cf. 2 Corinthians 10:5).

Fourth, the apologist must have the proper *goal*. His aim is to secure the unbeliever's unconditional surrender, without compromising his own fidelity to the Word of God.

The "word of the cross" must be used to expose the pseudo-wisdom of the world as destructive foolishness (1 Corinthians 1:18–19), and Christ must be set apart as Lord in one's heart (1 Peter 3:15), thus acknowledging no higher authority than God's Word, and refusing to suspend our intellectual commitment to the truth of that Word.

Apologetics: The Method

In light of the intellectual situation and these requirements for the apologist, let us finally consider what should be our procedure for defending the faith.

First, realizing that the unbeliever is "holding back the truth in unrighteousness," the apologist should *reject* the foolish presuppositions implicit in his opponent's critical questions and assertions, and instead attempt to educate him.

This will involve presenting the facts within the context of the biblical philosophy of fact. Notice we *do* present the facts — we are "evidentialists" — but we present them within a presuppositional framework where they make sense.

That framework is this: That God is the

sovereign determiner of all possibility and impossibility. A proper reception and understanding of the facts will require submission to the Lordship of Christ.

The facts will be significant to the unbeliever only if he has a presuppositional change of mind — from darkness to light — and Scripture alone has authority to declare what has happened in history, and to interpret what has happened.

Scripture not only declares the fact that Jesus rose from the dead (e.g., 1 Corinthians 15:3–4), but that he did so to secure our justification (Romans 4:25).

Next, the unbeliever's espoused presuppositions must be forcefully attacked. He needs to be asked whether knowledge is even possible given his espoused presuppositions. We must *demonstrate* that God has made foolish the wisdom of the world.

The believer should place himself, as it were, in the unbeliever's intellectual position, and proceed to "answer him according to his folly, lest he be wise in his own conceits." That is, we can demonstrate the outcome of unbelieving thought based on its own assumptions.

The unbeliever's claim should be reduced to impotence and impossibility by an internal critique of his system. We must demonstrate the ignorance of unbelief by arguing from the impossibility of anything contrary to Christianity.

During this dismantling, the apologist should be sure to appeal to the unbeliever as a true bearer of the image of God who has the clear and inescapable revelation of God available to him, thus giving him an ineradicable knowledge of his Creator.

This knowledge can often be exposed by indicating unwitting expressions in the unbeliever or by pointing to the "borrowed capital" (i.e., the unadmitted presuppositions that cannot be found in his philosophical system).

Finally, the apologist should declare the self-evidencing and authoritative truth of God as the precondition of all intelligibility and man's only way of salvation from all of the effects of sin, be they ignorance or intellectual vanity.

Lest the apologist become like the unbeliever,

he should not answer him according to his folly but according to God's Word.

The unbeliever should be invited to put himself on the Christian's intellectual foundation, in order to see that it alone provides the necessary grounds for intelligible experience and factual knowledge, thereby concluding that it alone is truly reasonable, and that it provides the very foundation for proving anything whatsoever.

Further, the apologist must show that Scripture accounts for the unbeliever's own state of mind — his hostility to God's truth and his refusal to acknowledge the necessary truth of God's revelation.

Scripture alone provides the only escape from the effects of this hostility and failure, be they intellectual futility or eternal damnation.

Apologetics: No Compromise

In conclusion, we must not compromise the faith in order to defend the faith. The Bible gives us an entire ontology (what is real), epistemology (how we can know), and ethic (how we should live).

In defending the faith, it is essential that we do justice to the Bible's whole teaching on the level of our apologetic presuppositions, as well as our apologetic methodology.

Our goal is not simply to defend an abstract system of thought, but ultimately — in the power of the Holy Spirit — to *persuade* men (2 Corinthians 5:11), and that persuasion comes from a faithful presentation of the truth, the whole truth, and nothing but the truth.

A WORD FROM THE
BAHNSEN INSTITUTE

The Bahnsen Institute exists to introduce a new generation of Christians to the work of the late Greg L. Bahnsen (1948–1995).

Dr. Bahnsen was a theologian, apologist, and ethicist whose ministry spanned the last quarter of the 20th Century. He received his theological training at Westminster Theological Seminary in Philadelphia, PA, and was granted his PhD in philosophy from the University of Southern California. Working within the Reformed theological tradition, he was a student and proponent of the "presuppositional" apologetic method pioneered by Cornelius Van Til.

His more academic books (*Theonomy in Christian Ethics* and *Van Til's Apologetic: Readings and Analysis*) are considered definitive in their fields by many, but more often than not, his writings — many of them published following his untimely death from complications of open-heart surgery in 1995 — are aimed at a popular audience.

Books such as *Always Ready: Directions for Defending the Faith*, *Presuppositional Apologetics: Stated and Defended*, and *Homosexuality: A Biblical View* have been of immense value to individual believers interested in thinking God's thoughts after him and living a consistently biblical ethical life.

Bahnsen was a minister in the Orthodox Presbyterian Church with years of pastoral and discipleship experience. He was always concerned to add the principles and methods of presuppositional apologetics — developed in the academic study — to the "toolbox" of every believer that was interested in giving a reason for the hope he or she has (cf. 1 Peter 3:15).

Accordingly, he was regularly found "taking it to the streets" (in the words of the popular song); holding conferences and seminars that were accessible to a wide range of Christians across the country and the globe. This little book is offered to the Christian public with that same desire.

Bahnsen was also interested to take the apologetic fight to the enemies of biblical faith — the proponents of naturalism, agnosticism, atheism, humanism, and those who practice the "ethics" of lawlessness. He was a bold and effective debater, and was willing to take on anyone who would engage.

As his reputation grew (especially after his debate with noted atheist Gordon Stein), the willingness of opponents to meet his challenges chilled considerably. In fact, one noted atheist even withdrew from an already-scheduled and advertised debate with Bahnsen.

Not only were these debates models for the deployment of presuppositional apologetic arguments, but God used them to embolden many Christians who had been intimidated by the bluster of the village atheist.

Thankfully, especially in view of Bahnsen's early death, much of his oral ministry at conferences, debates, seminars, and sermons has been preserved with audio recordings, which have been remastered and are available under the auspices of the Bahnsen Institute.

In the American evangelical world, "everything is debatable" and apologetical principles and methods are no exception. Even within the smaller world of "Reformed" theology and apologetics, the discussions between those who espouse the so-called "classical" model and "presuppositionalists" have been ongoing and oftentimes heated.

One of the most able and popular proponents of the "classical" approach was the late R.C. Sproul, founder and director of Ligonier Ministries.

In 1977, an exchange was arranged at Reformed Theological Seminary in Jackson, Mississippi between Dr. Sproul and Dr. Bahnsen, who was at the time a member of the faculty at the seminary. It is often referred to as a "debate," but it was more an informal, and extremely cordial, exchange of views between the two apologists.

Both men stressed the many theological assumptions they shared as heart-committed Reformed ministers. Further, the two agreed as to the goal of apologetics (i.e., to both defend the faith and persuade men).

Each offered a presentation, and the floor was then opened to the small audience of seminary

www.ingramcontent.com/pod-product-compliance
Ingram Content Group UK Ltd.
Pitfield, Milton Keynes, MK11 3LW, UK
UKHW030635040425
456976UK00007B/422

BE THE ANGEL
(INVESTOR)

BE THE ANGEL
(INVESTOR)

KEVIN JOHNSON

Contents

1

Introduction

Ever dreamed of getting in on the ground floor of the next big thing?

Picture this: you, playing a key role in shaping the future of innovation while (hopefully) watching your bank account grow. That's the magic of angel investing—where visionaries like you help turn bold ideas into world-changing realities.

This book is your backstage pass to the thrilling world of startup funding. By the time you're done, you'll have the know-how, strategies, and confidence to navigate angel investing like a pro. No fluff, no confusing jargon—just real, practical insights that would normally take years (and a few expensive mistakes) to learn.

You'll discover how to spot game-changing startups, negotiate deals like a seasoned investor, and build a portfolio that could lead to impressive returns. But beyond the money, angel investing is about being part of something bigger—a forward-thinking community of innovators shaping the future of business and technology.

Now, let's be clear: this isn't some "get rich quick" scheme. Angel investing takes guts, strategy, and a willingness to take calculated risks. That's why this book is packed with real-world examples, expert insights, and practical strategies you can start using right away. You'll learn from the successes (and failures) of others, giving you an edge in the game.

Imagine the thrill of discovering a startup with huge potential, mentoring ambitious founders, and watching your investment fuel the next big breakthrough. With the tools in this book, you'll be able to evaluate startups, gauge their potential to shake up industries, and make smart investment decisions.

By the end, you'll have a rock-solid understanding of how angel investing works. You'll be ready to step into the role of an angel investor—not just writing checks but offering valuable guidance and connections that help startups thrive.

Whether you're a seasoned entrepreneur or just dipping your toes into the startup world, this book has insights tailored to your journey. The road ahead is packed with excitement and opportunity. So, what are you waiting for? Turn the page and let's get started!

2

The Essence of Angel Investing

Angel investing stands as a beacon of opportunity in the vast sea of investment options. You've likely heard the term before, perhaps in hushed tones of excitement or with an air of mystery. But what exactly is angel investing, and why should you care?

At its core, angel investing is the practice of providing capital to early-stage startups in exchange for equity. You, as an individual with means and a passion for innovation, can become a key player in the growth of promising new businesses. This chapter will unravel the intricacies of angel investing, tracing its roots and illuminating its unique position in the investment landscape.

The Origins and Evolution of Angel Investing

The term "angel investor" has an interesting history. It originated in the early 20th century on Broadway, where wealthy individuals would provide financial backing for theatrical productions. These benefactors were seen as "angels" descending from above to save struggling shows. Fast forward to today, and the concept has evolved significantly. Modern angel investing took shape in the 1970s and 1980s as the technology boom created a new class of wealthy entrepreneurs looking to reinvest their success into the next generation of startups. You're part of this legacy when you step into the world of angel investing. It's a tradition of visionaries supporting visionaries, of experienced business minds nurturing the seeds of innovation.

While both angel investing and venture capital involve funding startups, they differ in several crucial ways. As an angel investor, you're typically investing your own money, whereas venture capitalists manage pooled money from many investors. Angel investments are usually smaller, ranging from $25,000 to $100,000, while venture capital firms might invest millions. This difference in scale affects the stage at which investments are made. You, as an angel investor, often get involved at the very early stages of a startup – sometimes when it's just an idea or a prototype. Venture capitalists, on the other hand, tend to enter the picture later, when there's more proof of concept and market traction. Another key distinction lies in the level of involvement. As an angel investor, you have the opportunity to be more hands-on, often acting as a mentor and advisor to the startup. Venture capital firms typically take a more formal approach, often securing board seats and having a say in major company decisions.

The Appeal and Myths of Angel Investing

So, why should you consider becoming an angel investor? The reasons are as diverse as the startups you might fund, but here are some compelling motivations:

There is potential for high returns, as a successful exit through an acquisition or IPO can multiply your initial investment many times over. It also offers portfolio diversification, allowing you to hedge against market fluctuations. Additionally, there is personal satisfaction in being part of a startup's journey from inception to success. Angel investing provides learning opportunities that expose you to new industries, technologies, and business models. It enables networking with other successful investors, entrepreneurs, and industry leaders. Lastly, there may be potential tax incentives, depending on your jurisdiction.

Angel investing, like any investment strategy, comes with its share of misconceptions. Let's address some of these myths head-on: First, angel investing is not only for the ultra-wealthy. While you do need to have a certain level of financial stability, you don't need to be a millionaire to become an angel investor. Many angels start with smaller investments and gradually increase their involvement as they gain experience. Second, while angel investing carries risks, these can be mitigated through careful due diligence, portfolio diversification, and ongoing education. The key is to approach it as a calculated risk rather than a gamble. Third, angel investors are not just in it for the money. While financial returns are important, many are equally motivated by the desire to mentor young entrepreneurs and contribute to innovation in their field of expertise. Lastly, you don't need to be a tech expert to be an angel investor. While many angel investments are in tech startups, there are opportunities across various industries. Your expertise in any field can be valuable to the right startup.

The Role of Angel Investors in the Startup Ecosystem

You might wonder where angel investors fit into the broader startup ecosystem. Think of the startup journey as a relay race, with different types of funding passing the baton at various stages.

In the seed stage, startups focus on product development and often have no revenue yet. This is where angel investors come in, providing the initial capital needed to turn ideas into reality. As the company progresses to the early stage, when initial growth begins and larger funding is required, angel groups and early-stage venture capital firms start getting involved. The growth stage sees significant expansion, attracting larger venture capital firms that invest heavily in scaling the business. Finally, in the late stage, when the company is preparing for an exit, private equity firms and corporate investors take over, leading the startup toward acquisition or an IPO.

Your role as an angel investor is crucial. You provide not just the initial capital that helps a startup get off the ground, but also the guidance and connections that can set it on the path to success.

The Changing Landscape and Future of Angel Investing

The world of angel investing is dynamic, constantly evolving with technological advancements and shifts in the global economy. Some trends shaping the future include the rise of crowdfunding platforms democratizing angel investing, increased syndication allowing for larger investments and shared due diligence, global reach breaking down geographical barriers, focus on impact investing seeking both financial returns and positive social or environmental impact, and efforts towards diversity and inclusion in funding a wider range of entrepreneurs.

As you consider stepping into the world of angel investing, it's important to prepare yourself. Start by assessing your finances to ensure you have the disposable income to invest without jeopardizing your financial stability. Define your goals, whether primarily seeking financial returns or also motivated by mentorship opportunities. Identify your expertise to guide your investment decisions. Build your network by attending startup pitch events and joining angel investor groups. Educate yourself through books, workshops, and courses on angel investing. Finally, start small with initial investments as you learn the ropes.

Legal and Ethical Considerations in Angel Investing

Being an angel investor means staying mindful of the legal and ethical responsibilities that come with the role. In many countries, including the United States, you need to meet certain financial criteria to be considered an accredited investor and participate in certain private investment opportunities. Due diligence is crucial, not only to protect your interests but also to ensure you're providing value to the startups you fund. Maintaining confidentiality is essential for building trust and protecting the interests of the companies you invest in. Be aware of potential conflicts of interest, especially if you're investing in multiple startups in the same industry or if you have other competing business interests. Lastly, consider the ethical implications of the startups you fund, ensuring they align with your values and will have a positive impact on society.

Wrapping up this introduction to angel investing, it's important to keep in mind that this is just the start of your journey. The world of angel investing is rich with opportunities for those willing to learn, take calculated risks, and support the next generation of entrepreneurs. In the following chapters, we'll dive deeper into the practical aspects of becoming a successful angel investor, equipping you with the knowledge and tools you need to make informed investment decisions and potentially reap significant rewards.

3

Inside the Mind of
an Angel Investor

Stepping into the shoes of an angel investor is like donning a pair of multifocal lenses. You're not just looking at numbers and projections; you're peering into the future, assessing human potential, and navigating a complex ecosystem of innovation and risk. This chapter takes you through the intricate thought processes, motivations, and responsibilities that define the angel investor's mindset.

The Angel Investor's Manifesto

At the heart of every angel investor lies a unique blend of visionary thinking, calculated risk-taking, and a desire to nurture innovation. You're not just writing checks; you're betting on dreams and backing the dreamers who dare to bring them to life. This role requires a delicate balance of optimism and pragmatism, coupled with a willingness to embrace uncertainty.

As an angel investor, you're often one of the first believers in a startup's potential. This early faith comes with immense responsibility and the potential for significant rewards. Beyond providing capital, you're offering validation, guidance, and sometimes a crucial lifeline to fledgling businesses at their most vulnerable stage. The potential for substantial returns is enticing—successful angel investments can yield returns of 10x, 20x, or even higher—but these high returns come with equally high risks.

Many angel investors are drawn to the opportunity to engage with cutting-edge ideas and technologies, staying at the forefront of innovation across various industries. For successful entrepreneurs turned investors, there is often a strong desire to "give back" to the startup ecosystem by sharing hard-earned wisdom and helping shape the next generation of business leaders. Angel investing also opens doors to a vibrant community of fellow investors, entrepreneurs, and industry leaders, creating valuable personal and professional connections. Additionally, angel investments can serve as a means of diversifying an investment portfolio beyond traditional stocks and bonds, potentially hedging against market fluctuations.

Some investors are motivated by a genuine interest in a particular industry or technology, allowing direct involvement in areas that excite them. Increasingly, angel investors also see their role as an opportunity to fund businesses addressing pressing social or environmental issues, combining profit with purpose.

The Art of Assessing Startup Potential

One of the most crucial skills you'll develop as an angel investor is evaluating startups. This process is part science, part art, and a healthy dose of intuition honed through experience. When assessing a startup's potential, several key factors come into play:

The Team: Often cited as the most critical factor, the founding team must be passionate, knowledgeable, coachable, and resilient. Their skills, experience, and dynamics can make or break a venture.

Market Opportunity: The size, growth potential, and competitive landscape of the market determine whether a startup is addressing a real, sizable problem.

Product-Market Fit: Does the product or service genuinely solve the problem it claims to address? Early traction or customer feedback can be indicative of future success.

Business Model: The startup must have a viable and scalable revenue model. Understanding how it plans to make money is crucial for long-term sustainability.

Competitive Advantage: What sets the startup apart? This could be proprietary technology, unique partnerships, or an innovative approach to solving a problem.

Traction and Milestones: Progress indicators such as early customers, revenue, or strategic partnerships can provide confidence in the startup's potential.

Exit Potential: While it may seem premature, considering possible exit strategies—acquisition, IPO, or other liquidity events—is vital for your return on investment.

Valuation: A reasonable valuation, given the startup's stage and potential, impacts your potential returns and its ability to raise future funding.

The Multifaceted Role of an Angel Investor

Your role as an angel investor extends far beyond providing capital. You'll find yourself wearing multiple hats, each crucial to the success of your portfolio companies:

- **Mentor:** Drawing from your own experiences, you'll guide entrepreneurs through the challenges of starting and scaling a business.

- **Connector:** Your network is invaluable, allowing you to introduce startups to potential customers, partners, and future investors.
- **Strategist:** You'll help shape the company's direction, offering insights on product development, market entry strategies, and growth plans.
- **Cheerleader:** Startups face numerous challenges, and your moral support can be crucial during tough times.
- **Gatekeeper:** Your investment and involvement lend credibility to a startup, opening doors to further funding and opportunities.
- **Risk Manager:** While embracing the inherent risks of early-stage investing, you also work to mitigate them through due diligence and ongoing involvement.

The Essential Skill Set of a Successful Angel Investor

To thrive in the world of angel investing, you'll need to cultivate a diverse set of skills:

- **Financial Acumen:** Understanding financial statements, valuation methods, and investment terms is essential.
- **Industry Knowledge:** A solid grasp of the sectors you invest in helps you make informed decisions.
- **Networking Skills:** Building and maintaining relationships with key players is crucial for sourcing deals and adding value to your investments.
- **Due Diligence Expertise:** A systematic approach to evaluating startups ensures informed investment decisions.
- **Negotiation Skills:** Agreeing on terms and helping your portfolio companies navigate partnerships can impact long-term success.
- **Emotional Intelligence:** The ability to read people, manage relationships, and provide

support during high-stress situations is invaluable.

- **Adaptability:** The fast-moving startup world requires comfort with change and uncertainty.
- **Pattern Recognition:** Over time, you'll develop the ability to spot trends and recognize successful patterns across different startups and industries.

Risk Management and Portfolio Diversification

Angel investing is inherently high-risk, high-reward. While the potential for significant returns is alluring, approaching it with a clear risk management strategy is crucial.

A portfolio approach is essential—diversifying across multiple investments can help mitigate risk. Determine how much you're willing to invest in total and in each startup. A common rule of thumb is to allocate no more than 10% of your investable assets to angel investments. Additionally, reserving capital for follow-on investments in your most promising startups can help maintain your equity stake as the company grows.

Thorough due diligence is your first line of defense against potential pitfalls. Develop a systematic process and don't skip steps, no matter how exciting an opportunity seems. Consider breaking your investment into tranches tied to specific milestones to manage risk and incentivize performance.

Investing alongside other angels or angel groups can help spread risk and leverage collective expertise in due diligence. Diversifying across different industries and regions further mitigates risk by tapping into diverse markets and innovation hubs.

The Psychological Side of Angel Investing

The journey of an angel investor is as much psychological as it is financial. You'll need to navigate a range of emotional challenges, including:

- **Dealing with Uncertainty:** The early-stage nature of angel investments means handling a high degree of ambiguity and change.

- **Managing FOMO (Fear of Missing Out):** The fear of missing the next big thing can lead to rushed decisions. Discipline is key.
- **Cultivating Patience:** Returns from angel investments take years to materialize, requiring a long-term perspective.
- **Handling Emotional Attachment:** While it's natural to become invested in startups, maintaining objectivity is crucial.
- **Coping with Failure:** Many investments will fail. Resilience and learning from failures are essential.
- **Balancing Optimism with Realism:** While optimism is essential in the startup world, it must be tempered with a realistic assessment of risks and challenges.

Conclusion

Success in angel investing is a journey of ongoing learning and adaptation. You're not just investing in startups; you're investing in your own growth as a savvy business mind and visionary thinker. The skills and perspectives you develop will serve you well beyond your investment portfolio, enriching your professional and personal life in unexpected ways.

4

The Investment
Process Decoded

From Pitch to Partnership: The Angel Investor's Journey

The path from spotting a promising startup to sealing the deal is a thrilling rollercoaster of decisions, risks, and—hopefully—big rewards. This chapter will guide you through every step of the angel investment process, equipping you with the knowledge and confidence to navigate this exciting world like a pro.

Finding the Diamonds in the Rough

Your journey begins with finding high-potential startups—a process known as deal sourcing. This is where both art and science come into play. Cast your net wide, but keep a sharp eye out for quality. Here's how:

- **Network, network, network** – Attend startup pitch events, entrepreneurship conferences, and industry meetups. You never know where you'll find the next unicorn.
- **Join angel groups** – Collaborating with other investors gives you access to a steady stream of vetted deals and the wisdom of experienced backers.
- **Leverage online platforms** – Sites like AngelList, Gust, and SeedInvest offer curated startup investment opportunities.
- **Engage with accelerators and incubators** – These organizations nurture early-stage startups and host demo days where you can see fresh talent.

- **Utilize professional networks** – LinkedIn, Twitter, and industry forums are goldmines for discovering new ventures.
- **Build your personal brand** – Position yourself as an expert and a supportive investor. When founders seek you out, you're doing something right.

Remember, quality beats quantity. Focus on startups that align with your expertise and interests. Not only will this increase your chances of success, but it will also allow you to add value beyond just writing a check.

Separating Promise from Hype

So, you've found some interesting startups—now it's time to separate the real gems from the shiny distractions. A compelling pitch should check these boxes:

- **Clear problem statement** – Does the startup solve a significant pain point?
- **Innovative solution** – Is it unique and better than existing alternatives?

- **Market opportunity** – How big is the target market, and can the startup realistically capture a slice?
- **Scalable business model** – Is there a clear path to profitability?
- **Traction and milestones** – Are there early customers, partnerships, or revenue streams?
- **Strong founding team** – Do they have the skills, passion, and adaptability to execute their vision?
- **Competitive advantage** – How does this startup stand out from the competition?
- **Financial projections** – Even if speculative, do they show an understanding of key growth drivers?
- **Exit strategy** – How could this investment eventually pay off for you?

Don't be dazzled by flashy presentations alone—dig deep and ask tough questions. Look for founders who are passionate but realistic. A great pitch is just the beginning; it's your job to uncover the real potential beneath the surface.

Conducting Due Diligence

Due diligence is where you separate fact from fiction. While the depth of your research depends on the size and stage of the investment, here are key areas to investigate:

- **The team** – Verify their professional history, education, and references.
- **Legal status** – Check incorporation documents, contracts, and any existing agreements.
- **Intellectual property** – If they claim proprietary technology or patents, confirm it.
- **Financial health** – Review financial statements, cash flow projections, and debts.
- **Market analysis** – Validate claims about market size, trends, and competitors.
- **Customer validation** – Talk to early customers or beta testers.
- **Technical review** – If it's a tech startup, consult an expert.
- **Regulatory compliance** – Ensure they have necessary licenses and meet industry regulations.

- **Past investors** – What's their experience with the company?
- **Reputation check** – Look for customer reviews and media coverage.

Due diligence isn't about looking for reasons to say no—it's about gathering the right information to make an informed decision. Be thorough, but respectful of the founders' time.

Negotiating Terms and Closing the Deal

If the startup checks out, it's time to talk terms. This isn't about squeezing every last cent out of the founders—it's about striking a deal that benefits everyone. Key elements to consider:

Term	Description	Why It Matters
Valuation	How much the company is worth	Determines your equity stake
Pro-rata rights	Option to maintain your ownership percentage in future rounds	Protects against dilution
Liquidation preference	Who gets paid first in an exit scenario	Shields you from downside risk
Information rights	Access to updates and financials	Keeps you informed
Board seats	Formal role in governance	Allows influence on big decisions

The negotiation process should be collaborative, not adversarial. You're in this together for the long haul, so align incentives from the start.

Once the terms are set, it's time to formalize the investment:

1. **Draft the term sheet** – A high-level summary of the investment terms.
2. **Review legal documents** – Get everything checked by a lawyer.
3. **Confirm due diligence items** – Any final questions?
4. **Obtain board approval** – If required.
5. **Transfer funds** – Making it official!
6. **Issue shares or investment instruments** – Your ownership is now on paper.

Use digital deal rooms for secure document sharing and e-signatures to keep things moving smoothly. Once the deal is closed, the real work begins.

Post-Investment Engagement: More Than Just Money

Closing the deal is just the start of your journey as an angel investor. Your ongoing engagement can significantly impact the startup's success—and your potential returns. Here's how you can help:

- **Regular check-ins** – Stay updated on progress and challenges.
- **Strategic guidance** – Offer insights and advice.
- **Networking support** – Introduce them to valuable contacts.
- **Recruitment assistance** – Help them find top talent.
- **Operational support** – Assist with scaling and efficiency.
- **Emotional support** – Startups are tough; be a trusted sounding board.
- **Future fundraising prep** – Help them gear up for the next round.

That said, don't micromanage. Support, don't control. Let the founders do their job while being available when they need guidance.

Legal and Tax Considerations

Don't let the fine print trip you up. Stay ahead of these key legal and tax implications:

- **Accredited investor requirements** – Know if you qualify.
- **Tax obligations** – Be aware of capital gains tax and investment deductions.
- **Securities laws** – Ensure compliance with regulations.
- **Confidentiality** – Keep sensitive startup info private.
- **Conflict of interest** – Avoid potential ethical dilemmas.
- **Record-keeping** – Maintain thorough documentation.

Consult with a startup-savvy attorney or tax professional to ensure you're in the clear.

Wrapping It Up: Your Angel Investing Adventure

Angel investing isn't just about making money—it's about being part of something bigger. You're helping shape the future of innovation, supporting bold ideas, and forming lasting partnerships.

By mastering each stage—from deal sourcing to post-investment engagement—you'll increase your chances of making smart, strategic invest-ments. And as you gain experience, your instincts will sharpen, making you an even more effective investor.

So dive in, embrace the journey, and enjoy the thrill of backing the next generation of game-changers!

5

Your First Investment

Congratulations! You've made it to the moment where talk turns into action—your very first angel investment. It's equal parts thrilling and nerve-wracking, but don't worry; we've got you covered. This chapter is your roadmap, guiding you through finding the right startup, conducting due diligence, negotiating terms, and making sure your investment doesn't just take off but soars.

Spotting a Winning Startup

Before you start throwing money around, you need to know where to look. Angel investing isn't about picking names out of a hat—it's about strategy, connections, and a keen eye for potential. Here's how to stack the deck in your favor:

- **Define Your Investment Criteria**: Decide on factors like industry, startup stage, location, investment size, and expected returns. Think of it as setting your "dating profile" for startups—you want the right match.
- **Tap Into Your Network**: Let people know you're looking! Your personal and professional circles can be goldmines of opportunities.
- **Attend Industry Events**: Conferences, startup meetups, and pitch nights are great places to meet ambitious founders.
- **Join Angel Groups**: These structured networks offer access to pre-vetted startups and wisdom from seasoned investors. Many let you observe before committing.

- **Explore Online Platforms**: Sites like AngelList, Gust, and SeedInvest curate startups actively seeking investment, making your search easier.
- **Engage With Accelerators**: These programs mentor early-stage startups and often host demo days showcasing promising ventures.
- **Build Your Brand**: Establish yourself as an investor and thought leader by writing, speaking, or posting on social media. The best deals often come to those who make themselves visible.
- **Track Your Leads**: Use a spreadsheet or CRM system to keep tabs on potential investments and their progress.

Evaluating a Startup Like a Pro

Once you've found a promising startup, it's time to put on your detective hat. Every founder will tell you their company is the next big thing—but your job is to separate hype from reality. Here's what to scrutinize:

1. **The Team**

People make or break a startup. Look for:

- **Industry experience**: Do they know their field inside out?
- **Balanced skill sets**: Do the founders complement each other's strengths and weaknesses?
- **Track record**: Have they built something successful before—or at least learned valuable lessons from failure?
- **Coachability**: Are they open to feedback, or are they stubborn to a fault?
- **Grit**: Can they handle the inevitable rollercoaster of entrepreneurship?

2. **The Market**

A great idea in a tiny market won't get you far. Assess:

- **Total Addressable Market (TAM)**: How big is the potential pie?

- **Serviceable Addressable Market (SAM)**: How much of that pie can they realistically capture?
- **Growth Rate**: Is the market expanding, stagnating, or dying?
- **Trends & Disruptions**: What could change the game for better or worse?

3. **The Product & Business Model**

- **Unique Value Proposition**: What makes them stand out from competitors?
- **Product-Market Fit**: Do they have traction, or is this still an untested idea?
- **Scalability**: Can this grow without costs ballooning?
- **Intellectual Property**: Do they have patents, trade secrets, or other competitive moats?

4. **Traction & Financials**

- **Revenue Growth**: If they're making money, is it increasing steadily?

- **Customer Retention**: Are people coming back, or is it a one-and-done deal?
- **Burn Rate & Runway**: How long can they survive before needing more cash?
- **Financial Projections**: Are their assumptions realistic or pure fantasy?

5. **Exit Strategy**

- **Acquisition Potential**: Who might buy them in the future?
- **IPO Possibility**: Could this company go public?
- **Exit Multiples**: What kind of return have similar companies delivered?

The Art of Due Diligence

Time to dig deeper. Due diligence helps you verify claims, uncover risks, and avoid costly mistakes. Here's how to do it right:

1. **Make a Checklist**: Cover key areas like legal structure, financials, intellectual property, team background checks, market validation, and competitive analysis.

2. **Request Key Documents**: Incorporation papers, cap table, financial statements, contracts, IP filings—get it all in writing.

3. **Talk to Stakeholders**: Interview founders, team members, customers, and even competitors.

4. **Do Independent Research**: Read industry reports, analyze competitors, check online sentiment.

5. **Bring in Experts**: Consider hiring legal, financial, or technical advisors to validate critical areas.

6. **Visit the Startup**: A firsthand look at their operations can reveal a lot about company culture and efficiency.

7. **Analyze Everything**: Cross-check information for inconsistencies and potential red flags.

The goal isn't to nitpick—it's to ensure you make an informed decision.

Structuring Your Investment Like a Pro

Now comes the negotiation phase. You want fair terms that protect your interests while ensuring the startup has room to grow. Key points to consider:

- **Valuation**: Ensure it aligns with comparable companies and growth potential.
- **Investment Vehicle**:
  - **Common Stock**: Simple but offers little investor protection.
  - **Preferred Stock**: More rights but adds complexity.
  - **Convertible Note**: Debt that converts to equity, delaying valuation discussions.
  - **SAFE**: A simple way to secure future equity.
- **Ownership Percentage**: How much of the company will you control?
- **Pro-Rata Rights**: Can you invest in future rounds to maintain your stake?
- **Board Involvement**: Do you want a formal role or just occasional updates?
- **Liquidation Preference**: Ensures you get paid first in case of an exit.

- **Anti-Dilution Protection**: Protects your ownership in case of a down round.
- **Founder Vesting**: Ensures they stick around for the long haul.

Negotiation is a balancing act. You're not just securing a good deal—you're forging a long-term partnership.

Closing the Deal & Beyond

Once terms are agreed upon, it's time to finalize the investment:

1. **Sign the Term Sheet**: This outlines the agreed terms before legal documents are drafted.
2. **Complete Due Diligence**: Tie up any loose ends.
3. **Get Board Approval**: If required.
4. **Transfer Funds**: Make it official!
5. **Receive Ownership Confirmation**: Stock certificates or investment agreements.

But your job doesn't end there! Post-investment, you can add value by:

- **Checking In Regularly**: Stay updated on progress.
- **Providing Strategic Guidance**: Offer insights when needed.
- **Making Introductions**: Connect them with potential customers, partners, or investors.
- **Helping With Hiring**: Great talent makes great companies.
- **Offering Moral Support**: Founders need encouragement just as much as funding.

Every investment is a learning experience. Keep a journal of what worked, what didn't, and how you can refine your approach for the next deal.

Final Thoughts

Making your first angel investment is a huge milestone. It's exciting, it's educational, and yes, it's a little nerve-wracking. But with a solid strategy, thorough due diligence, and a focus on long-term partnerships, you'll set yourself up for success. Embrace the journey, stay curious, and most importantly—enjoy the ride!

6

Recap and Next Steps

Standing at the threshold of your angel investing journey, you've gained a wealth of knowledge and insights. This final chapter serves as both a recap of essential takeaways and a roadmap for your continued growth as an angel investor. The road ahead is filled with opportunities, challenges, and endless potential for personal and financial rewards.

Key Takeaways from Your Angel Investing Journey

Angel investing is more than just a financial transaction—it's a partnership. As an angel investor, you fuel innovation, support ambitious entrepreneurs, and contribute to economic growth. Along the way, you've learned:

- **The Role of an Angel Investor:** Beyond providing capital, you offer mentorship, connections, and strategic guidance at a critical stage in a company's development.
- **The Psychology of Success:** Balancing optimism and pragmatism is essential. Taking calculated risks, maintaining a long-term perspective, and embracing resilience will help you navigate the uncertainties of investing.
- **How to Identify Promising Startups:** Leveraging your network, engaging with angel groups, and evaluating startups based on their team, market potential, product-market fit, and scalability will increase your chances of success.

- **The Importance of Due Diligence:** Thorough due diligence is your best defense against potential pitfalls. Understanding financials, verifying claims, and spotting red flags are critical skills.
- **Navigating Investment Terms:** Understanding term sheets and investment structures ensures you make informed decisions while balancing your interests and the needs of the startup.
- **Active Involvement:** Your role doesn't end with writing a check. Actively supporting your portfolio companies through mentorship and networking can significantly impact their success—and your returns.

Continuous Learning and Growth

Angel investing is a lifelong learning process. The startup ecosystem is ever-changing, and staying informed will keep you ahead of the curve. Here's how:

- **Stay Updated:** Follow industry publications like TechCrunch, VentureBeat, and AngelList Insights.
- **Attend Industry Events:** Conferences like the Angel Capital Association Summit and local startup events will expand your network and knowledge.
- **Join Angel Networks:** Organizations like the Angel Capital Association or European Business Angel Network provide deal flow, resources, and opportunities to co-invest.
- **Connect with Other Investors:** Peer discussions, investor meetups, and online forums offer valuable perspectives and shared learning experiences.
- **Take Courses:** Platforms like Udemy, Coursera, and the Angel Resource Institute offer structured learning programs.
- **Mentor Startups:** Engaging with entrepreneurs before investing helps sharpen your evaluation skills and provides deeper insights into the startup world.

Evolving Your Investment Strategy

As you gain experience, your approach will refine itself. Here's how to evolve your strategy:

1. **Adopt a Portfolio Approach:** Instead of hoping for one home run, diversify with at least 10–15 investments to spread risk.
2. **Develop an Investment Thesis:** Identify industries or trends that align with your expertise and interests.
3. **Specialize:** Deepen your knowledge in a specific sector to become a high-value investor in that space.
4. **Consider Follow-On Investments:** Supporting successful startups in later rounds can maximize returns.
5. **Explore Syndication:** Co-investing with other angels can reduce risk and enhance deal quality.
6. **Experiment with Investment Instruments:** Convertible notes, SAFEs, and equity investments each have unique benefits—choose wisely.

Measuring Success and Managing Expectations

Success in angel investing isn't just about financial returns. Consider these additional measures of success:

- **Learning and Personal Growth:** Every investment teaches valuable lessons.
- **Network Expansion:** Your connections with entrepreneurs and fellow investors open new opportunities.
- **Impact:** Supporting groundbreaking innovations creates meaningful change.
- **Entrepreneurial Support:** The guidance you provide can directly shape the future of promising startups.

Managing expectations is crucial—many investments will fail, but a few big wins can offset losses. Stay patient, keep learning, and refine your approach with each experience.

Navigating Challenges and Ethical Considerations

Every angel investor faces hurdles. Being prepared will help you navigate them effectively:

- **Balancing Involvement:** Support startups without micromanaging.
- **Emotional Resilience:** Failures will happen—learn from them and move forward.
- **Time Management:** Prioritize your investments wisely.
- **Avoiding Conflicts of Interest:** Stay transparent and ethical in all dealings.
- **Upholding Ethical Standards:** Align investments with your values and consider the impact of the businesses you support.
- **Maintaining Open Communication:** Transparency fosters trust and strengthens your relationships with startups and co-investors.

Embracing the Angel Investor Lifestyle

Angel investing is about more than money—it's about growth, impact, and engagement with a vibrant entrepreneurial ecosystem. To fully embrace this role:

- Attend startup events not just to invest but to contribute to the community.
- Share your experiences through speaking engagements or writing.
- Mentor entrepreneurs and guide the next generation of investors.
- Engage with incubators, accelerators, and universities to foster innovation.
- Align your investments with your broader values and goals.
- Give back by mentoring newer angel investors and advocating for startup-friendly policies.

Your Journey is Just Beginning

Every experienced angel investor was once a beginner. The knowledge, insights, and strategies you've gained are just the foundation for your journey ahead. The world of angel investing is rich with possibilities, and your role in it can be as impactful as you choose to make it.

This is just the beginning—the best is yet to come. Now, go out there and start investing!